You!!
Battling the Emotional Road

Turn It Around

by
Chris Bates

Bloomington, IN  Milton Keynes, UK

authorHOUSE™

AuthorHouse™
1663 Liberty Drive, Suite 200
Bloomington, IN 47403
www.authorhouse.com
Phone: 1-800-839-8640

AuthorHouse™ UK Ltd.
500 Avebury Boulevard
Central Milton Keynes, MK9 2BE
www.authorhouse.co.uk
Phone: 08001974150

First published by AuthorHouse 7/26/2006

ISBN: 1-4259-2444-1 (sc)

Printed in the United States of America
Bloomington, Indiana

This book is printed on acid-free paper.

Email: seabates@earthlink.net

Back cover photo done by Sharleen Apsey Middleville, Michigan.

Front cover sketch done by Jesse Heys Senior at Caledonia High School.

I would like to dedicate this book to God. He was able to show me a way to deal with each emotion by turning it around and making me stronger than I was before.

About the Author

When I reached the point where God became first in all I did, there was this peace that started to form. The struggles inside of me became less and less. The journey was not an easy one. My road was very difficult and at times still is, but I've learned in time how to get through it with His help. The one piece of great advice that I can give you is "HANG IN THERE." It may seem to be very discouraging, but you will make it. God was there for me and He will be there for you. If you've read my first book "You!!!! Can Walk the Road" then I can only hope at this point that you have found God and made Him a part of your life. Once I found that I needed Him, then the second battle began. The emotional battle. From leaving the old me to the new me. With God the choices on the outside got easier, but it's the emotional road on the inside that is very hard. I hope as you read this, that you will learn to turn each emotion around and focus on the opposite point instead. There is a positive side to each battle. I was taught once that as a thought enters the mind, it will enhance a feeling or emotion. Then from there starts a reaction. The stop sign needs to be put up right away after the thought enters the mind. Ask yourself what the thought is telling you? How do you feel? What is it telling you in your heart? Does it line up with Gods laws and ways? These are some of the questions you need to answer before it goes on. Don't let the wrong feeling take over and then turn into a bad reaction. Turn it to good and beat it. Winning the emotional battle is not going to happen overnight, but it will get easier in time if you stay determined. You are in my thoughts and prayers for the end to be victorious. Don't give up but find a way. Your relationship with yourself and with God will be so awesome.

Emotions to Battle

Afraid
Alone
Anxious
Backsliding
Bitter
Confusion
Denial
Despair
Doubt
Empty
Failure
Fears
Furious
Greedy
Guilt
Jealousy
Lost
Misery
Proud
Rebellious
Sorrowful
Stubborn
Troubled
Unbelief
Weak

Turning the Battle Around

Through each emotion there is a way to turn it around and focus on the opposite point. When learning to turn it, there is a way that God will play a role in helping you do this. Focus on Him because He is there to help you get through. You need to get from one side to the other. Seek which way!!!!!!!!!!

Afraid-Courage   (trust with both hands)
Alone- Companion   (let God inside of you)
Anxious-Calm   (ask God to show you)
Backsliding-Strong   (walk with God)
Bitter-Healing   (Gods guidance in revealing)
Confusion-Confidence   (ask God to help)
Denial-Accept   (right direction with God)
Despair-Persevere   (Gods strength that you need)
Doubt-Trust   (hand the heaviness over to God)
Empty-Fulfillment   (God back in my life)
Failure-Success   (God is leading a new way)
Fears-Accomplish   (God will be right there)
Furious-Forgiveness   (Gods lessons of life)
Greedy-Thanks   (thank God for what you have)
Guilt-Righteous   (your relationship with God grows)
Jealousy-Content   (blessings that God has given you)
Lost-Fullness   (God is trying to talk to you)
Misery-Happiness   (let God work in that spot)
Proud-Humble   (God gives you a talent)
Rebellious-Obedient   (Gods word teaches us)
Sorrowful-Joy   (God is never going to leave you)
Stubborn-Reason   (with God there will be this peace)
Troubled-Patience   (trust God and be patient)
Unbelief-Faith   (with God nothing is impossible)
Weak-Faithful   (being right in Gods eyes)

Afraid

Definition- frightened, fearful, filled with concern or regret

Psalm 56:11
In God have I put my trust and confident reliance; I will not be afraid. What can man do to me?

Being afraid. Each individual has it's own perspective of what scares them. From being a baby to an adult. We all have something that we are afraid of. How we handle each situation determines the outcome. When we are small we depend on adults to help us, but as we get older we depend less on adults because we became one. Now we rely on ourselves or listen to someone close to us that may have been through it already. In some cases that may help but if we rely on ourselves or others instead of letting God lead you through by giving you the strength and the wisdom to face it, then you may never get past what you're afraid of. We get stronger in life as we grow older by the lessons and events we experience. Trust God with both your hands to give you the courage that you need.

Opposite Point:
Courage- ability to conquer fear or despair

Psalm 31:24
Be strong and let your heart take courage, all you who wait for
and hope for and expect the Lord!

From the steps of a little child
one after another causes some fear
we grow up and reach further
moving through each event, life becomes more clear

Fear strengthens the heart
when you have courage and trust
some steps will cause you to fall
but you will arise and shake off the dust

With God on your side
from a child to an adult
you will trust and lean on him
your victory is in the vault

Alone

Definition- separated from others

Ecclesiastes 4:10
For if they fall, the one will lift up his fellow. But woe to him who is alone when he falls and has not another to lift him up!

You can sometimes rely on your friends or family too much. Whenever something goes wrong or you just don't want to be by yourself. There is going to be a point when nobody is going to be there and you will feel so alone. God is going to grab your hand and lift you up. He will give you whatever you need to get through. You will need to <u>let God inside of you</u> and work on where you are weak. If nobody is there don't ever think that you are alone. You don't need anybody to be with you. You have God with you all the time. Turn your life around and let Him in and you will have a companion for life.

Opposite Point:

Companion- one who accompanies or associates with another

Psalm 122:8
For my brethren and companions' sake, I will now say, Peace be within you!

You feel so alone and no where to go
there has always been someone near by
but this time they're busy and gone away
you will fall to your knees and cry

It's time to face this all by yourself
from the ground you will feel a hand
God's reaching out for you to grab hold
He'll lift you up, on your feet you will land

Feeling alone will slowly fade away
He's standing right next to you
whatever the situation you cross
His companionship and peace is with you

Anxious

Definition- uneasy in mind, worried

Matthew 6:34
So do not worry or be anxious about tomorrow, for tomorrow will have worries and anxieties of it's own. Sufficient for each day is it's own trouble.

Before each day ends there is a thought on the mind that torments you because you worry about what is going to happen. When you wake up the next day it appears before anything else. You just don't know what to do. You really can't concentrate on anything else because this has taken all your thoughts. Before you know it, you have thought yourself right into a disaster from thinking about it too much. When we become so wrapped up in the problem we lose sight of everything else. One of the things that you can do is STOP!! Take a deep breath and try to erase it from your mind a little until you have calmed yourself down. Look at the problem with a calm attitude and ask God to show you a way to solve it.

Opposite Point:
Calm- a condition free from storms, state of tranquility, stillness

II Timothy 1:7
For God did not give us a spirit of timidity (of cowardice, of craven and cringing and fawning fear), but (He has given us a spirit) of power and of love and of calm and well-balanced mind and discipline and self-control.

There isn't a day that goes by
we're not anxious in our mind
whether it is big or small
the answers are hard to find

We keep searching for a way
which will make us crazy or nuts
instead of remaining calm
the worry hits hard in the gut

Learning to ask God to show you how
He will take your troubles away
the pressure will be lifted
the calm and stillness will be there to stay

<u>Backsliding</u>

Definition- one who goes back or turns back

Proverbs 14:14
The backslider in heart (from God and from fearing God) shall
be filled with (the fruit of) his own ways, and a good man shall
be satisfied with (the fruits of) his ways (with the holy thoughts
and actions which his heart prompts in which he delights).

There are so many emotions and feelings that you will fight once you decide that you want to <u>walk with God</u>. Leaving the old life behind and starting a new one. Old habits are hard to break but you will have to determine which way you want to go. As you grow, your desires, morals, lifestyle will all change, but it is for the better. Making the right choices and being around the right people. You have to be strong in your decisions. If you feel like you're backsliding, then seek God for more power in yourself to fight it. Fight it and make it. You will find that the way you live will be so rewarding and satisfying.

Opposite Point:
Strong- powerful, firm, solid, not easily broken

Psalm 31:2
Bow down Your ear to me, deliver me speedily! Be my Rock of
refuge, a strong Fortress to save me!

To walk with God is the choice
you must stay on solid ground
let the old life go and bring the new
a meaning of life will be found

There are times when the heart will slip
know the difference between right and wrong
old ways are staring you in the face
don't think this battle is short, it's long

To fight every day from old to new
His power and strength is there
seek and ask and bring it on
the old is not an option, now you care

<u>Bitter</u>

Definition- extremely harsh or cruel, marked by intensity (as of distress or hatred)

Job 3:20
Why is light (of life) given to him who is in misery, and life to the bitter in soul.

Why am I filled with so much bitterness? You need to ask yourself that very question. What has got me so mad? What is the real source behind the way that I feel? The real problem is what you need to search for. Once you can narrow down what is really getting at you, then you can work on just that alone. It could be a lot of different things, but you need to figure out what the root of it is. Deal with the situation head on. It could be a person, something that happened to you a long time ago. Whatever has you distressed to cause you a lot of hatred, ask for <u>Gods guidance in revealing</u> the true source and also the guidance and strength to heal it.

Opposite Point:
Healing- curing, making whole or well

Psalm 147:3
He heals the brokenhearted and binds the wounds (curing their
pains and their sorrows).

Hatred that is found down in the soul
is formed from a deep rooted past
you have to deal with it head on
so the feeling will go away and not last

Bringing the bitterness to a head
and facing it with a healing heart
you can learn to let it go
the peace in you will begin to start

The peace that you get is real
from being bitter to a loving desire
with God as your guidance for strength
it will go out like the watering of a fire

Confusion

Definition- to make mentally unclear or uncertain

Psalm 71:1
In you, Oh Lord, do I put my trust and confidently take refuge;
let me never be put to shame or confusion.

I'm so confused!!! How many times have you asked yourself that question? Once you seem to get a handle on things and what you are supposed to do, WHAM. Life seems to put this extra little event in your path that makes you ask that question. There's a fork in the road and you have to decide which way. Before you put that foot down and make that decision, weigh out the end result. Is there a sign at the beginning of that road that helps? <u>Ask God to help</u> with a sign. Follow the arrow that points in the right direction. Trust God for the right arrow. Pretty soon your heart will know.

Opposite Point:
Confidence- trust, reliance, self assurance

Proverbs 3:26
For the Lord shall be your confidence, firm and strong, and
shall keep your foot from being caught (in a trap or some hidden
danger).

Most of everyone's day is set in stone
we have our routines of life to do
but before you know it, something happens
the feelings that come with it are new

Confusion sets in and questions start
you don't know how to handle it
emotionally it takes a lot of your thoughts
because it changes things and doesn't fit

To figure it out and make it more clear
ask for Gods help and seek the sign
the answers seem to appear before you
and you will know at that point everything is fine

Denial

Definition- refusal to admit the truth of a statement or charge

Matthew 26:70
But he denied it falsely before them all, saying, I do not know what you mean.

The defense side goes up. You're being accused of something. "I don't know what you mean" or "I don't do that". These are pretty normal statements that would come out. Facing reality about yourself is a hard thing to deal with, but it can be one of the best things that ever happens to you. It's between you and God or you and someone else. You're at the point that you have a choice to make on how you're going to handle it. You need to face and then repair the gap that has been made. Accepting the facts is one of the first steps to putting your life in the <u>right direction with God</u>.

Opposite Point:
Accept- to receive willingly, to agree to

Proverbs 19:20
Hear counsel, receive instruction, and accept correction, that you
may be wise in the time to come.

Your defense goes up with walls
saying "not me" is the first thing
God revealing or someone else
the pain inside is like a bees sting

You have to face and accept
the facts that are revealed to you
the choice that you take or make
which decision will you do

You have fixed and repaired the gap
with God you're on your way
putting Him first in your direction
facing who you are, you're proud to say

<u>Despair</u>

Definition- to lose all hope and confidence

Ecclesiastes 2:20
So I turned around and gave my heart up to despair over all the labor of my efforts under the sun.

If you have a hope and are very confident about the outcome, then you have this force in you that will keep pressing on. Then one day the hope begins to dwindle away because it is not happening. Now you begin to look at life in a different way and do not like what you see. At this point you need to find a new strength. It's <u>Gods strength that you need</u>. The end result is outweighed and won't let you give up. Search for Him and ask for the extra power to keep going. When you finally make it, then all of it was worth it. God can put this amazing power of strength in you as long as you seek and keep persevering with hope.

Opposite Point:
Persevere- to persist in spite of difficulties

Psalm 51:10
Create in me a clean heart, O God, and renew a right, persevering,
and steadfast spirit within me.

You're driving and can see the end
pressing on until it comes true
but the fire is dwindling away
it's taking too long and now you're blue

It is slowly fading away
and I don't like what I see
where do I get the strength
to continue with confidence in me

Pressing harder and looking for light
it is drawn from the power He gives you
ask for extra strength to press on
perseverance to the end, you will do

Doubt

Definition- an inclination not to believe or accept

Deuteronomy 28:66
Your life shall hang in doubt before you; day and night you shall
be worried and have no assurance of your life.

It's not going to happen, it's not going to happen, and it beats at the brain. With that attitude it won't. Your heart won't let it go but your mind keeps fighting. Stop the battle between your heart and your brain. Trust what God has placed in your heart. Stay on the confident side of it. You don't have as many doubts in our life as you do assurances, but the doubts weigh more than the rest. Hand the heaviness over to God. When you wake up take on the attitude that you will fight the doubt and replace it with trust and you will find that a different perspective will start to take over.

Opposite Point:
Trust- to place confidence, hope, depend

Psalm 71:5
For you are my hope; Oh Lord God, You are my trust from my youth and the source of my confidence.

If you had to make a list
put a check by the things you're sure
make another list of doubts
your mind would focus on the second for a cure

The second list is not as long
but takes more of your time and thought
check the first one and work on that alone
too many at one time, there's no lesson to be taught

If you believe in Gods strength
he will pour it on each doubt
have the confidence and trust with each one
each item on the list will have a new route

Empty

Definition- containing nothing, lacking value, force, sense, or purpose

Psalm 94:11
The Lord knows the thoughts of man, that they are vain (empty and futile-only a breath).

You're numb!!!!! No thoughts, just blank. No fire is burning anywhere. What's happening? Why is everything in life OK, but yet you feel nothing? There is a piece missing and you just can't seem to figure out what it is. What is it that you're searching for? What is my purpose? This piece is the link that will pull the rest of it together to make it all fit. There's this tug in my heart and it's coming from God. The missing piece!!!!!! I need to put <u>God back in my life</u> or start a relationship with Him for the first time. Replace the missing piece with God. You will find a lot of peace and fulfillment. It's time to connect all the dots of your life so the picture is complete.

Opposite Point:
Fulfillment- to put into effect, satisfy, to bring to an end

Psalm 57:2
I cry out to God Most High, Who performs on my behalf and
rewards me (Who brings to pass His purposes for me and surely
completes them).

You can't figure out why
you feel so empty and blank
life is complete in your picture
but the feeling in the heart sank

What is missing is not in plain sight
the feeling is coming from above
God is pulling on me to feel
the missing piece is His love

The relationship needs to begin
the purpose and link to the gap
fulfillment and peace to be found
life takes off, hold tight to the strap

Fears

Definition- terror, trembling, carefulness

Psalm 55:5
Fear and trembling have come upon me; horror and fright have overwhelmed me.

Standing on stage in front of a lot of people, starting a new job, blind date. These are just a few things that cause fear. What are your fears? One of the things that you need to do in your life is face them. Once you can get past some of them, then you can move on. Fear will stop you from accomplishing bigger tasks. To have the feeling inside of beating a fear can be so awesome. God will be right there when you go through your fear. One foot in front of the other and the victory is there. The help is there, just ask. He also knows your fears and wants to help. He knows you can get it done. Start the list and mark off all the accomplishments. You can do it!!!!!!!!!!!!

Opposite Point:
Accomplish- to bring to completion, achieve

Isaiah 55:11
So shall My word be that goes forth out of My mouth: it shall not return to Me void (without producing any effect, useless), but it shall accomplish that which I please and purpose, and it shall prosper in the thing for which I sent it.

You will have fears that will stop you
knowing is the first step to take
what you do to face each one
accomplishment could be at stake

Put one foot in front of the other
God will be right by your side
the strength you will feel to defeat
the journey could be narrow or wide

You will get this until the end
no more fears or battles to fight
the next step won't seem so hard
victory on the path is in sight

Furious

Definition- fierce, angry, violent

Proverbs 29:22
A man of wrath stirs up strife, and a man given to anger commits and causes much transgression.

I'm never going to speak to that person again!!! I'm going to pay them back for what they have done to me. Revenge will get you no where. The longer you stew on it, the more angry you become. How many times have you done something and regretted it? One of the worst things to do is to take action when the fire is burning strong. If you can get yourself to calm down and put it on the back burner for a little while, then look at the situation again. Your mind and thoughts will be a little more rational. In Gods lessons of life He will ask you not to handle whatever has come your way. Let Him take care of whatever justice needs to be done. You need to find a way to forgive and move on.

Opposite Point:
Forgiveness- to give up resentment of, pardon, absolve

Violence and anger come from the dark
and placed on the heart to pay back
but revenge is not for you to do
hand it to God wrapped in a tight sack

Having the faith to trust the justice
and finding peace with it inside
He will take care of the problem for you
anger will go out like the oceans tide

It may take a little while to let it go
but no regrets when you are done
forgiving the moment and laying it to rest
heaviness on the chest no longer weighs a ton

Failure

Definition- a lack of success

Psalm 38:10
My heart throbs, my strength fails me; as for the light of my eyes,
it also is gone from me.

    The spark, the drive, that one thing that motivates you. You work hard at it. You strive to achieve it. In just a short period of time it's all gone. Then the heart begins to beat so rapidly going faster and faster. Then those words come out. "I'm a failure!!!" Why? In some cases the flame goes out on it's own over a period of time because the feeling in the heart dies. Other things in life could play a role in that. Where we start at and where we end up could be two different places. Life may take you in a new direction. That place in life was not where you were meant to be. You didn't fail, <u>God is just leading you a new way</u>. He wants you somewhere else where you will have success. Listen to Him.

Opposite Point:
Success- prosperous results

Joshua 1:8
This Book of the Law shall not depart out of your mouth, but you shall meditate on it day and night, that you may observe and do according to all that is written in it. For then you shall make your way prosperous, and then you shall deal wisely and have good success.

This one thing in life you drive for
you work hard and strive to see
it will pay off if this is your place
success or failure, which will it be

Failure is not a slap in the face
lives and events can change the heart
finding out that this is not your spot
feel inside which way you are throwing the dart

If you're throwing the dart at a certain thing
Gods guidance will help it land
it will hit the target where it's suppose to be
the spot you hit will have success that's grand

<u>Greedy</u>

Definition- selfish desire beyond reason

Proverbs 28:25
He who is of a greedy spirit stirs up strife, but he who puts his trust in the Lord shall be enriched and blessed.

You've got a great job, but it's not enough. You've got a nice house, but it's not big enough. It doesn't matter what you have, it has to be more. You're never satisfied with what you have. There is this desire to have more and more. The one thing you could ask yourself is if it all disappeared, would it matter? Are you a materialistic person? If you keep trying to get more, than you could be affecting everyone around you because you're probably going after it at whatever cost. Then one day it could be gone. Wanting more is OK but are you giving <u>thanks to God for what you have</u>? Do you stop and look and realize what's already there? Do you see the blessings before you?

Opposite Point:
Thanks- an expression of gratitude

I Chronicles 29:13
Now therefore, our God, we thank You and praise Your glorious
name and those attributes which that name denotes.

You have all these things in life
from a house to a car and more
even the best you've ever had
at what cost to open the next door

The door could cost you everything
does it matter if it all went away
there are so many blessings in front of you
do you notice or go on your way

Stop and look and realize what's there
thank God for all the big and the small
wanting more than what you really need
greediness can cause you to fall

Guilt

Definition- a feeling of responsibility for wrongdoing

Psalm 69:5
Oh God, You know my folly and blundering; my sins and my guilt are not hidden from You.

When something you did is wrong, you are left with this heavy feeling of guilt. It torments you terribly. It will constantly bother you because you know deep inside that it wasn't right. From this point on you need to find a way to repair what you did. Facing it and fixing it is something that a lot of people avoid. Not dealing with the truth about yourself. As your relationship with God grows, you will find yourself searching for the right way all the time. Fix the past, forgive them, ask for forgiveness and move on. From this point on you will know what to do and not to do. This will include relationships, careers, and everything else that plays a role in your life.

Opposite Point:
Righteous- acting or being in accordance with what is just, honorable, and free from guilt or wrong

Psalm 32:11
Be glad in the Lord and rejoice, you (uncompromisingly) righteous
(you who are upright and in right standings with Him); shout
for joy, all you upright in heart!

What you have done will eat away
and will mess you up inside
weighing heavy and with lots of guilt
reality in yourself, there's nowhere to hide

Face it and fix it is really hard to do
repairing the damage that's done
learning from the mistakes you made
you won't do it again and run

This is a lesson we all need to learn
to know about doing right not wrong
Gods laws are written for us to know
the righteous will be happy and strong

Jealousy

Definition- state of being jealous (intolerant of rivalry)

Proverbs 27:4
Wrath is cruel and anger is an overwhelming flood, but who is able to stand before jealousy?

There are people that you watch on TV or in your own lives that you are very jealous of what they have. You ask yourself "Why them and not me?' "I seem to always struggle." The question that you need to ask yourself is "Do I have any control over the situation that I am in?" Another perspective to look at is that you probably have more than a lot of people. Our lives are where they are for a reason and a lot of it is by choice. You need to find a way to be content with what you have and understand why you are where you're at. Other people are where they are at for a reason. Instead of looking at what someone else has, look at the blessings that God has given you.

Opposite Point:
Content- to be pleased or satisfied with present conditions
or state of being

Philippians 4:11
Not that I am implying that I was in any personal want, for I
have learned to be content (satisfied to the point where I am not
disturbed or disquieted) in whatever state I am in.

We all have a spot in life to be in
if with control or not at all
you make a choice to change it
or deal with where you were thrown the ball

Some places are not by choice
but you're there for reasons unknown
you may figure out some day and ask why
how come me and not them with a moan

Somebody will have something you don't
but they will be missing something you've got
Gods blessings come in all sorts of ways
if you counted them all, you would have a lot

<u>Lost</u>

Definition- unable to find the way

II John 1:8
Look to yourselves (take care) that you may not lose (throw away or destroy) all that we and you have labored for, but that you may (persevere until you) win and recieve perfect reward (in full).

You just don't know what is happening. Why do you feel so lost. You can't seem to get a grip on yourself and where you are suppose to go. You feel that everything you put your mind to doesn't work. This is when you need to get inside of yourself and listen to what is being said. <u>God is trying to talk to you</u>. You may be walking down the right path but your motives or how you are doing it may be all wrong. Step back, be still, and listen to what He's telling you. ASK!!!! Search for the answer. Is this what, where, and whom you need to be? This may be where your suppose to be, but you need to change a little or a lot. The fullness of it will show up. You will find your way.

Opposite Point:
Fullness- filled, complete, possessing or containing an abundance

John 1:16
For out of His fullness (abundance) we have all received (all had a share and we were all supplied with) one grace after another and spiritual blessing upon spiritual blessing and even favor upon favor and gift (heaped) upon gift.

> You are unable to find your way
> nothing seems to be going right
> you press on and on to get there
> but you keep stumbling day and night
>
> You feel so lost and can't get a grip
> but this path is the way you know
> each log that you trip and fall over
> questions come and you feel so low
>
> Instead of asking, stop and listen
> God's trying to talk and get it out
> He's giving gifts and blessings beyond
> the fullness you win with no doubts

Misery

Definition- emotional distress

Job 7:3
So am I allotted months of futile (suffering), and (long) nights of misery are appointed to me.

It is pretty much like the title of the book wrapped up into one word. The emotional distress that we battle. Misery is most of them all into one word. Any circumstance can fall into misery. What is the root of the misery? Find it. A dream, a job, family. Lots of different reasons. This is the battle you have to win to get some peace back in your life. God wants us to have joy and peace in our lives. Misery has to be fixed in the heart and turned to happiness. How? Ask yourself if it is something that you have control of. If it is out of your control then you need to <u>let God work in that spot</u> in your life.

Opposite Point:
Happiness- a state of well-being and contentment

Psalm 144:15
Happy and blessed are the people who are in such a case; yes,
happy (blessed, fortunate, prosperous, to be envied) are the people
whose God is the Lord.

We all have the battles
that can fulfill the misery sign
from one emotion to the next
we still find ourselves on a fine line

The root of the problem
is what you need to search for
finding a way to turn it around
deep in the heart is the core

From being miserable to happy
is the line you need to follow
let God work in that spot if needed
the hole in the heart is no longer hollow

Proud

Definition- having or showing excessive self-esteem, arrogant

Psalm 138:6
For though the Lord is high, yet has He respect to the lowly (bringing them into fellowship with Him); but the proud and haughty He knows and recognizes (only) at a distance.

You can walk through life with the feeling of great accomplishment. You worked your tail off to get where you are at. Did you know that <u>God gives each of us a special talent</u>, whether it may be writing, singing, sports, or even being a great mom that takes care of her kids? Each of us has something we will do in this life. Have you ever thanked God for what you are doing? Having God in your life brings out these gifts. Without God you could be doing something with no passion in it. With Him there and guiding you, you could end up somewhere you never thought you'd be and love it. Let Him show you where you need to go. Humble yourself and thank Him every day for what you are able to do.

Opposite Point:
Humble- to destroy the power or prestige of

Psalm 34:2
My life makes it's boast in the Lord; let the humble and afflicted
hear and be glad.

Whatever it is that you do in life
is the passion of the heart there
do you hate every day the door opens
and know there is not an ounce of care

The gift that God gives us to do
you should have Him right by your side
if the care is gone and so is the love
let Him guide you to your ultimate ride

Thinking where you're at, you got on your own
and not even acknowledging a thank you
God will watch you from a distance
until you humble yourself and realize from who

Rebellious

Definition- resistance to authority, insubordinate

Isaiah 50:5
The Lord God has opened My ear, and I have not been rebellious
or turned backward.

You have reached a point that you know that God needs to be a part of your life. You start reading the bible and you find yourself changing inside. The way that you handle things. Look at yourself a long time ago and now. How are you dealing with situations that you come across? Are you getting very angry or are you keeping more self-control? Learning the bible and applying it. Learning to be obedient and not going back to the old way is a huge step. Gods Word teaches us how to live, act, and decide what we are going to do. What you do with the Word is the question!!!!! Be obedient and follow the Word. There will be so much peace.

Opposite Point:
Obedient- to obey

Romans 6:17
But thank God, though you were once slaves of sin, you have
become obedient with all your heart to the standard of teaching in
which you were instructed and to which you were committed.

The missing piece you need to have
is the presence of God in your day
start at the beginning and read the Word
He will teach you and it will stay

As the words come across and sink in
your life will begin to change in your head
from the old ways applied to the new
the rebellious side will go dead

Make a commitment to obey and follow
from the dark to the bright of a light
may you never turn back or fall down
in your heart you will do what's right

Sorrowful

Definition- deep distress, sadness

Psalm 69:29
But I am poor, sorrowful, and in pain; let Your salvation, O God, set me up on high.

There are a lot of things that can cause deep sadness. Losing a loved one, financial disaster, or relationships ending. One thing that you can be sure of is that <u>God is never going to leave you</u>. He is always with you. In the beginning of the relationship with God you're going to go through a deep sadness of having to deal with your past life and the sins you've committed. The same sense of moving on, but you can't until you deal with this. Reach deep down in your heart and just ask. "God please forgive me for all my sins." Once you have dealt with this than there will be this overwhelming joy. Having Him with you all the time helps you to deal with anything that may cause sadness.

Opposite Point:
Joy- a source of happiness

Psalm 16:11
You will show me the path of life; In Your presence is fullness of
joy, at Your right hand there are pleasures forevermore.

You will reach a point of being sad
when a person or thing comes to an end
but moving on and putting it behind
comes a time when the heart needs to mend

Not everything is going to be there for life
you will go through some sort of loss
but the one thing you can be sure of
God is always with you, that you won't want to toss

He will be with you through everything in life
if you choose to have Him by your side
ask for forgiveness and let the past go
the joy you will be on will be an overwhelming ride

Stubborn

Definition- done or continued in a willful, unreasonable, or persistent manner, not easily controlled

Deuteronomy 9:13
Furthermore the Lord said to me, I have seen this people, and behold, they are stubborn and hard.

Your husband, your children, family, and friends. You will always find that one person who is so stubborn, or do they say that about you? It doesn't matter what the subject is about, but as long as there is a compromise made. You cannot keep standing firm on everything. The relationship will end up being torn apart over something that may be very small. Once you have a strong relationship <u>with God there will be this peace</u> that comes over you. Things that you were stubborn about before won't matter as much. There is always a way to settle whatever the issue may be. Find a way to reason with that person or in yourself to make the matter resolved.

Opposite Point:
Reason- to talk with another to cause a change of mind

Daniel 4:36
Now at the same time my reason and understanding returned to
me; and for the glory of my kingdom, my majesty and splendor
returned to me, and my counselors and my lords sought me out; I
was reestablished in my kingdom and still more greatness (than
before) was added to me.

Is there a stubborn one in the crowd
or is it the one looking in the mirror
whether it's a subject that is small or big
lowering the wall will cause a little fear

The wall comes down to draw you closer
to finding a solution and settling it
there is always a middle ground to meet
learn to bite your tongue a little bit

Situations before you felt a certain way
His peace makes compromise so nice
relationships stay strong and form real bonds
life is smooth like the rolling of the dice

Troubled

Definition- to agitate mentally or spiritually, disturb, worry

Psalm 25:17
The troubles of my heart are multiplied; bring me out of my distresses

You try not to worry about it, but end up driving yourself nuts thinking about it. What's going to happen, when, and why or who? These are all the questions that end up sometimes putting you over the edge. Everything in life happens for a reason. You need to put your <u>trust in God and be patient</u>. This is very hard to do. You will even try to do other things to keep your mind off of it. It will work for a while but you will still come back to it. Having patience doesn't happen overnight. You have to keep working at it. If it is meant to be, it will work itself out. One thing that will help is to pray and ask. Somehow the answer will appear, you just don't know when.

Opposite Point:
Patience- bearing pains or trials without complaint, showing self-control

James 1:3
Be assured and understand that the trial and proving of your faith bring out endurance and steadfastness and patience.

When is it going to happen
the waiting is making me insane
questions are there with no answer
the strength of patience, I need to gain

Patience and self-control is hard
things in life happen for a reason
trusting God and know that in time
he will bring it in to your season

You will never know the timetable
but trust, pray, and wait to see
let go of all the trouble and worry
He will bring to all you are to be

Unbelief

Definition- lack of faith, distrust

Romans 11:20
That is true. But they were broken (pruned) off because of their unbelief (their lack of real faith), and you are established through faith (because you do believe). So do not become proud and conceited, but rather stand in awe and be reverently afraid.

To walk through life not knowing that God loves you and is there for you is probably the strongest of all unbeliefs. You can even not believe in yourself and have the confidence to do what is placed in your heart to do. He loves you no matter who you are, no matter what you have done. You need to trust that He is there for you. Believe in yourself. <u>With God nothing is impossible</u>. If you set your mind to it and the desire is there, ask God and trust and have faith that it will come to pass. You're never alone, He's always with you. Your past is that, the past. Build a strong relationship with God now. It's never too late to start over and begin the right journey.

Opposite Point:
Faith- complete trust

I Corinthians13:13
And so faith, hope, love abide (faith-conviction and belief
respecting man's relation to God and divine things; hope-
joyful and confident expectation of eternal salvation; love-true
affection for God and man, growing out of God's love for and
in us), these three; but the greatest of these is love.

To not believe in God or even yourself
is the biggest part that needs to heal
it doesn't matter what the past holds
love in the heart, you have to feel

Nothing with Him is out of reach
the size doesn't effect it at all
faith and trust inside of you
with God, no order is too tall

Building a great relationship with Him
being alone is gone away from you
the journey is real and full of love
the amazement of what He will do

<u>Weak</u>

Definition- not able to resist much pressure, lacking strength or vigor

Matthew 26:41
All of you must keep awake (give strict attention, be cautious and active) and watch and pray, that you may not come into temptation. The spirit indeed is willing, but the flesh is weak.

Knowing the difference between right and wrong, and making the right choice. These are hard ways to live by if you are searching to <u>be right in Gods eyes</u>. Reading the Word every day and applying it. Leaving the old life behind and starting a new journey. He gives you guidelines and laws to make you a better person. You will come across paths of the old you and it will be very difficult to let it go, but you will. Your flesh is weak to the ways of the world. You have to go with what is right in your heart and right with God. He will make you stronger in that area if you ask. Focus on resisting and winning.

Opposite Point:
Faithful- loyalty, belief and trust in God

Matthew 25:21
His master said to him, Well done, you upright (honorable, admirable) and faithful servant! You have been faithful and trustworthy over a little; I will put in charge of much. Enter into and share and joy (the delight, the blessedness) which your master enjoys.

You don't want the old life
it is hard to move on and let go
but reading the Word every day
gives guidelines for you to know

Applying them to your life
and being right in Gods eyes
will be rewarding down the road
knowing in your heart you'll be very wise

To beat the desires of the weak flesh
and walk the path of the new way
baby steps at first grow into more
your faithfulness to God will stay

<u>Final Thought</u>

When I wrote this book 6 months ago, I did not have a final thought added to the book. Now I am in the final editing of this book and felt that this was a huge piece that was missing. I cannot express to you the emotional victories that I have had. In just 6 months time, the Lord has worked very hard with me to work through each battle and I have been very successful. The way that I felt then and the way that I feel now is two different worlds. It takes time so please don't feel that your situation is going to heal overnight. Continue to seek the Lord with each battle and you will find a victorious landing. Life is not perfect by any means, but you can work to be the best you can be at everything you do. Your feelings with events that come into your life will be handled so much better once you start working on dealing with things the right way. My perspective of life and my purpose has grown tremendously since this book developed. I pray that when you finish this book it will give you insight as to how life needs to be addressed as you cross paths with people and on your personal road.

I am working on a third book and it deals with a poetic route with people, places and the personal side of life. The name of this book is called "Lord let me see...Let me be". You will continue the sentence with the poem and it will relate to a moment in time that you are in.

God Bless You